HOW THEY
LIVED

A FAMILY IN
THE THIRTIES

SUE
CRAWFORD

Illustrated by
John Haysom

HOW THEY LIVED

Book Editor: Marcella Streets
Series Editor: Amanda Earl

First published in 1988 by
Wayland (Publishers) Limited
61 Western Road, Hove
East Sussex BN3 1JD, England

© Copyright 1988 Wayland (Publishers) Limited

British Library Cataloguing in Publication Data
Crawford, Sue
A family in the thirties – (How they lived)
1. Great Britain – Social life and
customs – 20th century – Juvenile
literature
I. Title.   II Haysom, John.   III. Series
941.083   DA566.4

ISBN 1 85210 604 2

All words that appear in **bold**
in the text are explained in the
glossary on page 31.

Typeset by Kalligraphics Limited, Redhill, Surrey.
Printed and bound in Belgium by Casterman S.A.

CONTENTS

HARD TIMES

The children peered out of their bedroom window as their father joined the march for jobs which stretched down the street below. The marchers were hungry and tired and the police were worried that a fight might break out. Suddenly an angry struggle erupted between the men at the head of the crowd and the police. Two policemen moved forward. Arms waved wildly, people were knocked to the ground and slogan boards were hurled through the air.

It was 1936 and millions of people in Britain were unemployed due to a worldwide **recession** called the Depression. Many workers accepted wage-cuts rather than risk losing their jobs; some were on such low wages they could hardly afford to feed or clothe their families.

It was a time of great hardship for families in industrial areas, such as Wales and the north of England. However the thirties was also a **decade** of great excitement. Those families with enough money spent it on new types of entertainment, such as buying a radio and going to the

cinema, or 'picture palace' as it was called. Meanwhile there were rumours that King Edward VIII wanted to marry Mrs. Simpson, who had been divorced twice. People were terribly shocked!

In these pages you will discover how ordinary families lived and how their lives changed during the thirties.

4

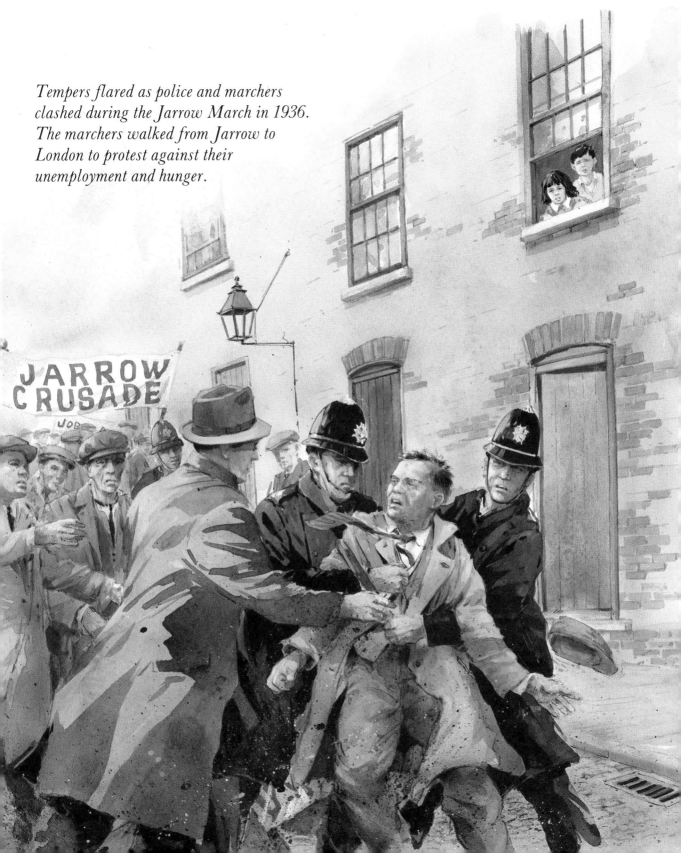

Tempers flared as police and marchers clashed during the Jarrow March in 1936. The marchers walked from Jarrow to London to protest against their unemployment and hunger.

WORK AND UNEMPLOYMENT

During the thirties there were important changes for people at work. Industries such as cotton, iron and steel had always needed to be near coalfields for power. Most of these were in the north of England. However, the new power of electricity meant that manufacturing companies sprang up in the south of England and there were interesting new jobs, for example designing, making and selling cars and electrical goods.

Those who kept their jobs in the old industries faced hazards such as coal dust, which damaged their lungs, and injury from heavy machinery, as there were few safety measures. Miners' families dreaded hearing the siren that warned them there had been a pit accident, as so many men were killed each year.

In shops and offices, conditions improved over the decade. Even without qualifications, a boy or girl who did well could work their way up to a high position in a company. The average weekly wage for a man in 1938 was £2 13s 3d (£2.66). However a woman earned on average only half of that, even for doing the same work! Those who wanted a good job could pay to learn shorthand and typing and become secretaries.

Unemployment was high. In 1932, almost three million people were

The switchboard and typewriter used by this secretary were considered modern in the thirties.

Above *For some, the misery of years of unemployment, hunger and poverty was difficult to bear.*

registered as unemployed and three times that number were too poor to afford proper food and housing. Government inspectors visited the homes of anyone requesting 'dole' money (**unemployment benefit**) and if they had anything that could be sold to raise money, their dole was stopped. Many people thought this 'means test' was unfair. A couple with four children would have been allowed up to £1 11s 3d (£1.56) a week on the dole, but would have needed 7–15 shillings (35–75p) per week for rent and 4 shillings (20p) for heating.

Below *Thirties coins. Top left to right: penny ($\frac{1}{3}$p), threepence ($1\frac{1}{4}$p), half-crown ($12\frac{1}{2}$p); bottom left to right: shilling (5p), silver threepence, farthing ($\frac{1}{12}$p), half-penny ($\frac{1}{6}$p).*

FAMILY LIFE

Some workplaces did not allow women to keep their jobs once they were married, so many women had to stay at home. Men were not expected to help with housework – their role was to earn enough money to keep a wife and children. The husband took all the family's major financial decisions, such as buying a house, while women controlled the household budget.

In the thirties, lessons were given to girls on how to be a good mother.

However, during the thirties, more and more young couples moved away from their families and the places where they had grown up, to try to find work. Because of this, husbands began to get more involved in caring for the house and children. Family planning clinics, such as those started by Marie Stopes, advised on **contraception**. By planning smaller families of two or three children, people could spend more money on each child.

Although it was less common than

before the First World War (1914–1918), wealthy families still employed servants such as a cook, a maid, a **chauffeur**, and a nanny to look after the children.

Good manners were thought to be very important in the thirties and children were often punished. If they were disobedient or rude to adults, they were sometimes beaten with a slipper and sent to bed hungry!

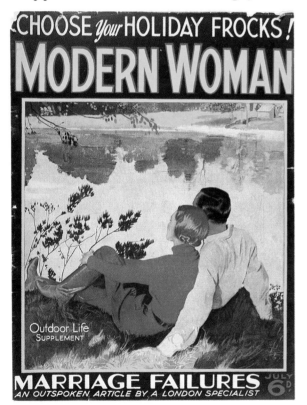

Like some magazines today, in 1935 Modern Woman *gave advice on home, fashion and marriage.*

Above *Many families still lived in poor conditions at the beginning of the thirties. Some families had to cook, eat and sleep in just one room.*

Children were not allowed as much freedom in the evenings as they are today and even thirteen-year-olds had to be in bed by about eight o'clock! Poor families often had only one bed for all their children; sometimes three children would sleep head-to-toe in one bed.

A HOUSE IN THE SUBURBS

In those city centres which were hit hard by the Depression, many homes were unhealthy slums. Large families often shared only one or two rooms, with no bathroom or running water and only an outside lavatory.

Below *In the thirties, many poor people did not have running water in their homes and so they had to fetch water from a pump in the street.*

As councils gradually cleared the slums away, they replaced them with more modern blocks of flats.

Between 1919 and 1939 four million new houses were built in Britain. Most were **semi-detached** and

A typical thirties suburban house.

built on estates in the suburbs of large towns. Many still exist today, with their large bay-fronted windows and 'pebbledash' walls.

For the first time ordinary families were able to borrow money through a **mortgage** to buy a home of their own. As house prices ranged from £400 to around £1,500, it was almost as cheap to buy as to rent. By the

An example of the type of bedroom furniture found in the new semi-detached suburban homes.

end of the thirties, 30 per cent of families in Britain owned their own homes, compared with only 10 per cent in the early twenties.

By the mid-thirties the national electricity grid had been completed so most new houses had electricity. Coal-fired boilers provided hot water but it was a hard and dirty job relighting them. Central heating was

rare. A labour-saving kitchen was one with fitted cupboards and tiling around the sink!

The latest homes were designed by the followers of a famous Swiss architect called Le Corbusier. These 'modern movement' houses had concrete walls, long metal-framed windows that curved around the corner of the house, and flat roofs.

This flat-roofed house in Saltdean, Sussex was built in the 'modern movement' style of the famous Swiss architect, Le Corbusier.

IDEAL HOMES

Compared with today there were few labour-saving machines in the thirties, although electric lighting made homes brighter than the old, dim gas lighting. Fridges and washing machines were rare. Clothes had to be washed by boiling and stirring them in a 'copper', which was a large tank with a fire burning underneath. Few people had vacuum cleaners, so floors and furnishings had to be cleaned by scrubbing. Keeping a home clean and looking after a family took much longer than today and women often had to work at this from dawn to dusk.

Like today, women's magazines in the thirties offered advice on everything to do with housekeeping and raising a family. It was fashionable to have few ornaments or pictures, and to tidy things away into cupboards rather than have them on show. Everything had to be 'modern'

Keeping a home clean, and looking after a family, was hard work without the labour-saving machines of today.

Labour-Saving Devices Which Save Both Time and Money

Please state Voltage when Ordering

REPAIRS

If it is anything Electrical write or 'phone Harrods

Prompt and highly skilled attention

EL 5702 'MAGNET' COOKER
For a family of 4-6 persons. Cast iron door, door frames, hot table, etc., and with sheet steel body. There are 2 enclosed boiling plates, and a griller or toaster, spacious oven Total loading 5,500 Watts. The oven and boiling plates are controlled by switches giving full, half and quarter heat. Price £18 0 0

Write for booklet showing full range of models

E 60 MAGNET ELECTRIC OSCILLATING FAN
Bracket or Desk type An exceptionally powerful type of Fan which can be adjusted according to requirements £5 18 0

NEW MODEL THE 'THOR' ELECTRIC WASHING MACHINE
An electric Washer and Wringer combined. Clothes can be thoroughly washed in the New 'Thor' Model in from 3 to 5 minutes, and the running costs are so low as to be almost negligible £29 17 6
Complete with Ironing Attachment £30 17 6

Complete booklet of Washing Machines forwarded on application

E 66 MAGNET ELECTRIC FAN
Desk or Bracket type, with current consumption of 34 watts £4 6 6
State Voltage when Ordering

EL 555 'PROTOS' ELECTRIC FLOOR POLISHER
For cleaning and polishing Linoleum, Parquet Floors, and Painted Floors. 2 brushes covering 12 ins. of floor Price complete with 23 ft cord, plug adapter, and 1 set of polishing brushes £13 13 0
Other makes in stock

HOOVER
The Greater Hoover. Model 700 . . . . £17 17 0
A more popular priced Hoover Model (541) £18 18 0
Dusting tools for both models £3 0 0
Either may be had for £1 down Only the Hoover embodies the exclusive deep-cleaning principle of Positive Agitation. Hangings, carpet, upholstery, are cleaned easier, quicker and more thoroughly
Supplied with new Floor Polishing Attachment £2 0 0 extra

EL 28 MAGNET ELECTRIC WASHING MACHINE
Washing day without labour. Saves time and money Washes 6 sheets or their equivalent in 15 minutes £42 0 0
Attachments are available for the machine so that it can be used for making ice-cream, mincing and sausage making, knife cleaning, making butter, etc.

EL 71 MAGNET ELECTRIC MASSAGE VIBRATOR
This is a valuable appliance, whether for medical use or simply as a toilet vibrator. The equipment includes six different types of applicators. Price £4 15 0

Left *The electrical appliances in this catalogue were too expensive for most people to buy.*

Above *This 1935 radio, or 'wireless set', is made of an early type of an early type of plastic called bakelite. Bakelite was made into all sorts of household goods, such as door handles.*

and '**streamlined**' – these were the catch-phrases of the day.

Advertisements tried to make the housework seem more attractive by suggesting that the latest cleaning products worked 'scientifically'. They showed happy families living in sparkling, perfectly tidy homes – not at all like the bustle and muddle of normal family life!

An early type of plastic called bakelite was made into all sorts of household products, from radios to combs. You can see these in junk shops today. Anything Victorian, such as floral designs on soft furnishings, was seen as old-fashioned. The latest style was stripes and jazzy zig-zagged patterns. Rooms were often decorated in pale 'peppermint' green, as this was the most fashionable colour of the time.

SHOPPING

People bought their food at small corner shops, as supermarkets did not exist. Look at the prices of the food. Potatoes cost only 2¼d (1p) per pound and bread 4¾d (about 2p) a loaf! Biscuits were weighed out on scales.

In the thirties a row of high street shops looked very different from the shops we are used to today. Instead of supermarkets there were many more small local shops. Few people had fridges to keep food fresh, so it was necessary to shop for such things as milk and butter several times a week. These **perishable** foods had to be kept in ice, bought from the fishmonger, or in a cool larder.

In shops, food was kept behind the counter. As the shop assistants knew most of their local customers, shopping was a friendly business. Dried goods such as biscuits, raisins and flour did not come in packets but were weighed and wrapped in paper in the shop. Housewives could order their shopping and have it delivered.

There were no frozen foods and the only **convenience foods** came in tins and jars. Jam, pickles, corned beef and condensed milk were particular favourites.

The Co-operative Stores ('Co-ops') shared their profits with the customers by giving **dividends** to regular shoppers. These could be exchanged for luxuries without dipping into the housekeeping money.

For home furnishings and clothes, people usually shopped in department stores, or made their own. There were usually three or four stores in a medium-sized town.

Food could be ordered from a shop and delivered by an errand boy.

Uniformed men in vans delivered people's purchases, as few women owned or drove cars. During the thirties shops began to allow customers to buy on hire purchase or 'HP'. For a small deposit people could obtain goods to use immediately and pay off the balance gradually. Obviously, this was very tempting! Sometimes people got into debt; then they borrowed money from a pawnbroker, who would keep their valuables, such as jewellery, in case they could not pay back the loan.

DIET AND HEALTH

Families on a reasonable income ate four meals a day. A cooked breakfast was followed by lunch – the main meal of the day – which consisted of meat and two vegetables plus dessert. Afternoon tea included sandwiches and cakes. Fish, egg or meat salad was served for supper. Tea was the main drink for rich and poor, and few people drank coffee.

Spotted dick was a popular pudding.

A typical cheap diet was made up of porridge for breakfast; bacon or sausages with root vegetables, followed by rice pudding, for lunch; and bread and margarine for tea. Fish and chip shops provided a cheap and nutritious form of take-away. However the very poor ate only bread and margarine. This led to **malnutrition**: thousands of poor children developed **rickets**.

Britain did not have the benefit of the wide variety of settlers and visitors from overseas that it has today and so many of the foods we eat now were not available. Families ate more sweet than spicy food, and as a result many people worried about their weight. Some even took harmful drugs to help them slim.

Families also began to take an interest in the vitamins and minerals needed for a correct diet. However smoking was not seen as a health risk. Children were given **laxatives** to keep them healthy and they dreaded visiting the dentist, as fillings were done without an injection!

Health was generally poor: in 1931

a man could expect to live for only about 59 years and a woman for around 63. (In 1980 the average was 71 for males and 77 for females). There was no National Health Service so most visits to the doctor cost money. Families who could afford it often joined an insurance scheme in case they needed treatment, but many poorer people simply did not call the doctor until it was too late.

Right *Exercise kept children fit.*

Below *Children who had been ill sometimes received sun-ray treatment to help them recover.*

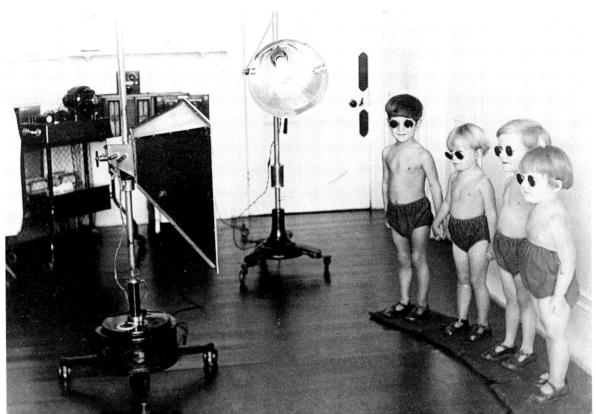

FASHION

Compared with the exotic fashions of the 1920s, the clothes worn in the thirties were more tailored and elegant but much plainer. Hemlines on women's skirts fell below the knee, jacket lapels were wide and exaggerated. Men's trousers were baggy and had turn-ups. Twin-sets (knitted cardigans over matching sleeveless tops) were more fashionable than jumpers for women. Clothes were generally much more **formal** than they are today.

People felt it was important to be dressed correctly. A man did not like to be seen in just his shirt sleeves and always wore a jacket and tie when he went out. Hats and gloves were worn for all occasions. Men wore trilbies or bowler hats. The fashion was to tilt your hat over one eye, perhaps to imitate a favourite Hollywood filmstar.

Girls wore pinafore dresses, while boys were often dressed in short trousers until their teens. Even poor families tried to keep one outfit, called their 'Sunday best', for going to church, but often they had to manage with second-hand clothes.

Many women had hand or treadle

Left *These baggy trousers with turn-ups, worn by Arsenal footballer Eddie Hapgood, were very fashionable in the thirties.*

Above *These 1937 dress patterns, free with* Ladies' Journal, *show the tailored, close-fitting styles popular at the time. Note the hats and hemlines.*

sewing machines and could turn out stylish clothes. Electric sewing machines were expensive so few families had one. Knitting was such a popular hobby that young children had to wear knitted woollen shorts, which could be most uncomfortable! Those who could afford it had their clothes specially made for them by tailors.

As well as the traditional materials of cotton and wool, clothes were beginning to appear in the new man-made fabric of rayon, which was a type of artificial silk.

Below *Children had little say in what they wore. Often they were dressed in uncomfortable knitted underwear, woolly shorts or skirts and jumpers.*

SCHOOLS

By the middle of the thirties all children had to go to school from age 5 to 14. Most children went to mixed council schools which were divided into three classes: infants, juniors and seniors. Senior boys had a separate playground from the senior girls, who had to share one with the juniors and infants. In the playground, games such as skipping and

School playtime could be spent skipping with a rope.

Classrooms were very formal. Each child had his or her own desk and was expected to study quietly.

hopscotch were played. Few schools had playing fields.

Lessons were given in reading, writing and arithmetic. Boys also learned science and woodwork, while girls were taught cookery, laundry and needlework. It was not thought suitable for boys to learn to sew or girls to make furniture. Many men grew up unable to cook themselves a meal.

From 11 to 18 years, children could go to grammar schools. Although fees were charged, bright children could take an entrance

During the thirties, children were given a small bottle of milk during their morning break at school.

exam to win a free place. However most children had to leave school and find work at 14. Those wanting to learn a skill, such as plumbing, became **apprentices** and paid for evening classes out of their wages.

Children whose parents could afford a private education were often sent to all-male or all-female boarding schools. Preparatory schools were for children age 5 upwards and public schools from age 14 to 18. As well as the subjects taught at ordinary schools, children learned Latin and Greek and were encouraged to play sports. It was difficult to go to university unless you had been to such a school (or you were rich).

At most schools, teachers were called 'Sir' or 'Miss'. Uniform had to be worn: gymslips for girls and shorts for boys – even for seniors! Grammar, poetry and times tables were learned off by heart and chanted aloud. Discipline was very strict and children were caned if they broke a school rule or were late – even if they had to walk 8 kilometres to school each day!

TRANSPORT

Cars were an expensive luxury at the start of the thirties and there were few on the roads. By the end of the decade a new car cost around £100 and a second-hand one could be as cheap as £10, so one in ten families in Britain owned a car. Although cars, coaches and lorries gradually replaced trams and horse-drawn vehicles, in some country districts a horse and cart was still used for local transport and deliveries, of milk, for example.

Most cars being driven were British-made, such as the Vauxhall Big Six, Austin Cambridge, Morris Minor and Hillman Minx. Black was the most common colour and cars had none of the extras we are used to today, such as stereos and seat-belts. Few cars even had heaters – in winter the driver and passengers wore a blanket over their feet to keep them warm.

So many road accidents happened during the early thirties that signs such as this had to be posted as part of the 1934 road safety campaign.

A driver did not need to pass a driving test and no MOT (Ministry of Transport) certificate was required, so many cars were very scruffy and dangerous. Some had an old armchair where the proper seats had been! There were so few rules of the road that, as traffic increased,

more and more accidents occurred. In 1932 there were almost as many fatal road accidents as in 1982, when there were ten times as many cars on the roads. Driving and walking were made safer by the introduction in 1934 of traffic lights, one-way streets, roundabouts, pedestrian crossings and a 30 mph (48 kph) speed limit in towns.

For families who moved out of cities to the suburbs, the steam train or the new underground tube offered

Below *The driver of this car is being taught by a Royal Automobile Club instructor how to teach others to drive, although there were no driving tests in the thirties.*

Above *As this poster shows, people who moved to the suburbs of London could travel to work by the underground.*

the ideal way to travel into the city each day to work. Even the smallest village near a railway line had its own station. Some of these trains were very fast: in 1938 'The Mallard' set a world record of 203 kph.

23

HOLIDAYS

Before 1938 only a quarter of the working population received a paid holiday each year. The rest had to manage without pay if they took any time off. Then a law was passed forcing all employers to give their workers a week's annual paid leave. Those families who could afford to go away often chose a **boarding house** on the coast. Only the wealthy

Airlines arranged holidays by 'flying boat'. These could land on water.

went abroad and they usually travelled by ship. Aircraft were such a new invention they were mainly used by the army and VIPs. One type of plane used for holidays was the 'flying boat', which could land on water. This plane was much more roomy than ours today, with armchairs, proper tables and beds!

Getting out in the fresh air became very popular during the thirties. At weekends the whole family might set off in the new car for a picnic in the countryside or a visit to the sea. Skegness, Brighton, Blackpool, Ayr and Rhyl were fashionable seaside resorts for daytrippers. On Bank Holidays the train stations swarmed with people queuing for trips organized by the railway companies.

A holidaymaker called Billy Butlin thought that there was so little to do on boarding house holidays if it rained, that in 1936 he opened the first holiday camp at Skegness. Swimming, organized games, competitions, cinema, ballroom dances, meals and accommodation were all included in one basic price at Butlin's

Above *Day trips to seaside resorts became popular during the thirties. People often dressed quite formally on the beach.*

– about £2 or £3 a week per person.

People of all ages joined clubs to go hiking, cycling or camping. 'Keep fit' was a catch-phrase of the day and the government tried to organize local sports and exercise days to keep everyone healthy.

Right *For £2 to £3 each per week, this couple spent their holiday at Billy Butlin's holiday camp in Clacton, which opened in 1938.*

HOME ENTERTAINMENT

In 1936 the first regular public television service was broadcast from Alexandra Palace. However few families had the chance to enjoy it in its first years, as television sets were extremely expensive. Instead people looked to their church and friends for entertainment far more than they do today. **Amateur** dramatics was a popular pastime for some, and for couples ballroom dancing was a fashionable way to spend the evening. Sons and daughters of wealthy people were

Dance halls were a favourite meeting place for young people.

These children are playing 'oranges and lemons', a traditional British game popular in the thirties.

encouraged to meet up at the tennis club or go to afternoon tea dances, so they would not be out late at night.

People also got together in each other's homes to play card games or sing around the piano. For poorer families, games and sing-songs took place in the local pub, although there were still many pubs just for men where women were not at all welcome.

By the end of the thirties the wireless, as the radio was called, had become the most popular home entertainment. A radio was quite expensive, costing around £20, but, along with the **gramophone**, radios soon replaced pianos as the main form of family entertainment. The only radio company, the BBC, tried to broadcast something for each member of the family – classical music, **jazz**, sport, education, drama, comedy, Children's Hour (presented by 'Uncle Mac'), and news programmes.

Live news and sports coverage was perhaps the most amazing thing about the radio. Listeners could sit in their living rooms and share in the excitement of test match cricket or a day at the races. For the first time, people could experience news as it was being made.

Children were usually left to play by themselves in the streets, as there were no such things as 'leisure centres' or 'adventure playgrounds'. Simple, popular games included 'hoop-la' (a game played with wooden hoops), and leap-frog.

The first television sets were quite large and transmitted pictures in black and white only.

PICTURE PALACES

In 1927 films with sound-tracks replaced silent movies and a trip to the cinema became a good way to forget the problems of the Depression. Spending an evening in a 'picture palace', as the cinema was called, was often warmer and more comfortable than staying at home, as the seats were large, well-padded and luxurious. Even a medium-sized town had four or five cinemas, and it only cost between sixpence (2½p) and 1 shilling (5p) for a ticket.

Audiences packed the cinemas for Laurel and Hardy films: they made

Tarzan, Jane and Boy star in Tarzan's Secret Treasure.

Thirties cartoon favourites: Snow White (left), Pluto and Mickey Mouse (right).

51 films in the thirties. Slapstick humour was very popular and American stars, like the Marx brothers, were loved by all. Singing cowboys such as Hopalong Cassidy were a favourite with older viewers in the mid-thirties, along with westerns such as *Stagecoach* starring John Wayne (1939) and romances like *Gone with the Wind* (1936). A fine story with romance, some humour, and plenty of action was the key to a good thirties film. As well as its westerns, the Hollywood film studios released 70 new musicals in 1930. In 1935 *Becky Sharp*, the first live action film to be made in 'technicolor', was released.

For children Walt Disney cartoons, such as *Snow White and the Seven Dwarfs* (1937), were favourites. Mickey Mouse, the star of the first cartoon to have words and music, was a household name. Some of the Tarzan films on television today were first shown in the thirties.

THE THREAT OF WAR

One way the government helped to create jobs during the thirties was by building aeroplanes and ammunition in case of another war. As the decade wore on, families everywhere began to fear that Germany's Adolf Hitler was planning war with Britain.

By the end of the thirties Britain was over the worst of the Depression. More people had jobs and many families had a home of their own, electricity and a car. Their lives had been changed by holidays, cinema and radio. Conditions for the poor were gradually improving as slums were pulled down and more and more schools and hospitals were run by the government. Although Edward VIII had **abdicated** in 1936 to marry Mrs Simpson, there were joyful celebrations throughout Britain when his younger brother, George, was made king. Nevertheless the decade ended uneasily, with many young men leaving home and loved ones, as their fathers had done twenty-five years earlier, to fight in World War II.

With the threat of war looming, children were taught how to use gas masks in case gas bombs fell on Britain.

GLOSSARY

Abdicated   Gave up a position of power.

Amateur   A person who takes up something as a pastime rather than as a paid job.

Apprentices   People who are learning a trade.

Boarding house   A house where you can rent a room and have meals.

Chauffeur   A person employed to drive a car for someone else.

Contraception   Something which prevents women becoming pregnant.

Convenience foods   Foods that are packaged so they store well and can be served easily, for example tinned goods.

Decade   A ten year period. The years between 1930 and 1940 are the decade known as the thirties.

Dividends   Profits made by the 'Co-op' stores, shared out to its customers in the form of tokens or stamps allowing discounts on food from the same store.

Formal   Proper; keeping to customs.

Gramophone   An early type of record player.

Jazz   A type of music and dance.

Laxatives   Medicine given to make you go to the toilet.

Malnutrition   Illness caused by poor diet and not enough food.

Mortgage   A promise that a property will be given back to the bank or building society that lent the money for it, if the loan cannot be repaid.

Perishable   Something which will rot quickly.

Recession   A time when business affairs in a nation are bad and many people do not have jobs.

Rickets   A common illness of the thirties caused by lack of Vitamin D, which led to softening of the bones and often bow legs or knock knees.

Semi-detached house   A house joined to another on one side only.

Streamlined   Shaped to move quickly or to look smooth.

Unemployment benefit   Money people receive from the government when they are out of work.

MORE BOOKS TO READ

Pascall, Jeremy, *The Cinema Greats* (Wayland, 1983)

Purkis, Sallie, *Home, the Town and Work in the 1930s* (Longman, 1984)

Quinney, Anthony, *House and Home* (BBC Publications, 1986)

Sichel, Marion, *Costume Reference 1918–1938* (Batsford, 1979)

Unstead, R.J., *The Thirties* (Macdonald, 1985)

Wilkins, Frances, *Transport and Travel from 1930 to the 1980s* (Batsford, 1985)

INDEX

Picture acknowledgements
The pictures in the book were supplied by the following: Aquarius Picture Library 28; BBC Hulton cover, 6, 7 (top), 10 (right), 15, 22, 23 (left), 25 (top), 26 (top and bottom) 27; Barnaby's Picture Library 8, 17 (top); Dr. Barnardo's 17 (bottom), 19 (right), 20 (top and bottom), 30; John Frost's Historical Newspapers 9 (left), 19 (left); Geffrye Museum 13 (right); Mary Evans 13 (left), 16; Paul Seheult 11 (right); Popperfoto 18, 25 (bottom); Royal Mint 7 (bottom); Topham Picture Library 9 (right), 10 (left), 11 (left), 21, 23 (right), 24; Walt Disney 29 (right and left).